PRIMARY
MATHEMATICS 6A
WORKBOOK

Marshall Cavendish
Education

US Distributor

SM Singapore Math Inc.®

Original edition published under the title Primary Mathematics Workbook 6A

© 1984 Curriculum Planning & Development Division

Ministry of Education, Singapore

Published by Times Media Private Limited

This American Edition

© 2003 Times Media Private Limited

© 2003 Marshall Cavendish International (Singapore) Private Limited

© 2014 Marshall Cavendish Education Pte Ltd

Published by Marshall Cavendish Education

Times Centre, 1 New Industrial Road, Singapore 536196

Customer Service Hotline: (65) 6213 9444

US Office Tel: (1-914) 332 8888 | Fax: (1-914) 332 8882

E-mail: tmesales@mceducation.com

Website: www.mceducation.com

First published 2003

Second impression 2004

Third impression 2005

Reprinted 2006 (twice), 2007, 2008, 2009 (twice), 2010, 2011,
          2012 (twice), 2014, 2015, 2016, 2017

Singapore Math Inc.®

Distributed by
Singapore Math Inc.®
19535 SW 129th Avenue
Tualatin, OR 97062
U.S.A.
Website: www.singaporemath.com

Marshall Cavendish is a registered trademark of Times Publishing Limited.

Singapore Math® is a trademark of Singapore Math Inc.® and
Marshall Cavendish Education Pte Ltd.

ISBN 978-981-01-8516-9

Printed in Singapore

ACKNOWLEDGEMENTS

Our special thanks to Richard Askey, Professor of Mathematics (University of Wisconsin, Madison), Yoram Sagher, Professor of Mathematics (University of Illinois, Chicago), and Madge Goldman, President (Gabriella and Paul Rosenbaum Foundation), for their indispensable advice and suggestions in the production of Primary Mathematics (U.S. Edition).

CONTENTS

EXERCISE 1

1. A watermelon weighs *m* kg and a pineapple weighs 2 kg.
    (a) Express the total weight of the fruits in terms of *m*.

    (b) If *m* = 4, find the total weight of the fruits.

    (c) If *m* = 6, find the total weight of the fruits.

2. Sumin bought a pen and a book for $*x*. The pen cost $5.
    (a) Express the cost of the book in terms of *x*.

    (b) If *x* = 11, find the cost of the book.

    (c) If *x* = 15, find the cost of the book.

3. Meihua bought 3 T-shirts at $n each.
   (a) Express the total cost of the T-shirts in terms of n.

   (b) If $n = 8$, find the total cost of the T-shirts.

   (c) If $n = 10$, find the total cost of the T-shirts.

---

4. The total height of 4 girls is w cm.
   (a) Express their average height in terms of w.

   (b) If $w = 592$, find the average height of the girls.

   (c) If $w = 608$, find the average height of the girls.

5. Find the value of each of the following expressions when $n = 15$.

(a) $n + 7$
 	
  $=$
	(b) $20 - n$
	
	  $=$

(c) $3n$
 	
  $=$
	(d) $n + 5$
	
	  $=$

(e) $\dfrac{n}{5}$
 	
  $=$
	(f) $n - 3$
	
	  $=$

(g) $\dfrac{n}{3}$
 	
  $=$
	(h) $5n$
	
	  $=$

(i) $3 + n$
 	
  $=$
	(j) $\dfrac{n}{45}$
	
	  $=$

EXERCISE 2

1.   Peter bought 6 mangoes at $x each. He also bought a papaya for $5.
     (a) Express the total cost of the fruits in terms of x.

     (b) If x = 2, find the total cost of the fruits.

     (c) If x = 3, find the total cost of the fruits.

---

2.   Vivian bought 6 bottles of cooking oil. She gave the cashier $40 and
     received $y change.
     (a) Express the cost of 1 bottle of cooking oil in terms of y.

     (b) If y = 10, find the cost of 1 bottle of cooking oil.

     (c) If y = 1, find the cost of 1 bottle of cooking oil.

3. Find the value of each of the following expressions when $k = 6$.

(a) $\dfrac{5k}{3}$ $=$	(b) $\dfrac{15 - k}{3}$ $=$
(c) $\dfrac{8 + k}{7}$ $=$	(d) $10 - \dfrac{2k}{3}$ $=$
(e) $\dfrac{k}{3} + k$ $=$	(f) $k - \dfrac{k}{6}$ $=$
(g) $k^2 + 4$ $=$	(h) $50 - k^2$ $=$
(i) $k^3 - 100$ $=$	(j) $3k^2 + 20$ $=$

EXERCISE 3

1. Simplify each of the following expressions.

(a) $x + x + x$ =	(b) $y + y + y + y$ =
(c) $2n + 3n$ =	(d) $p + 5p$ =
(e) $4x - x$ =	(f) $5y - y$ =
(g) $8p + p + 2p$ =	(h) $7e - 3e - 2e$ =
(i) $a + 4a - a$ =	(j) $5k - k + 2k$ =

2. Simplify each of the following expressions.

(a) $5n - 3n + 4$ =	(b) $6 + 5a - 3$ =
(c) $7x + 2 + 2x$ =	(d) $4a - 2a + 5$ =
(e) $4d + 6 - 4$ =	(f) $18 + 6f - 9$ =
(g) $12 + 8h - 6h$ =	(h) $9a + 1 - 3a$ =
(i) $7 + 4k - 2 - 2k$ =	(j) $15x + 8 - 10x - 3$ =

EXERCISE 4

1. Match the figures with the solids.

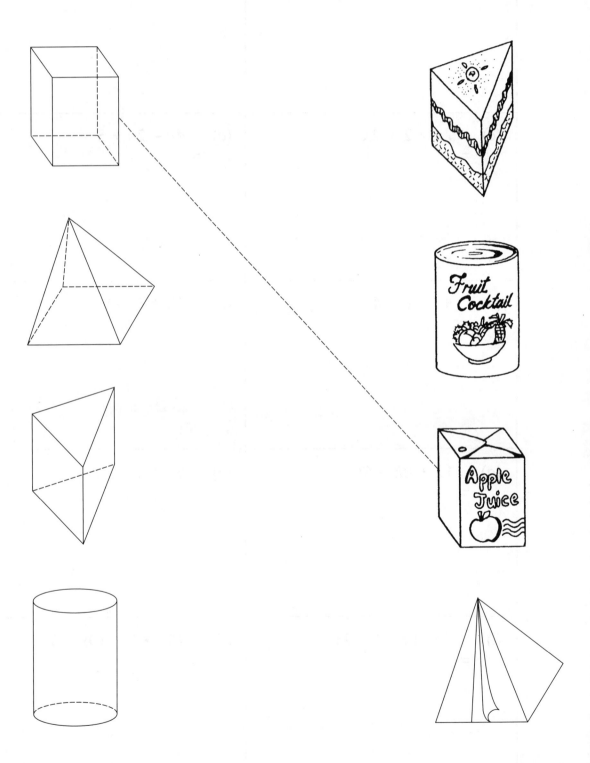

2. How many faces does each solid have?

Solid	Number of faces
(a)	
(b)	
(c)	
(d)	

EXERCISE 5

1. Which of the following can be folded to form a cube? Circle the letters below them.

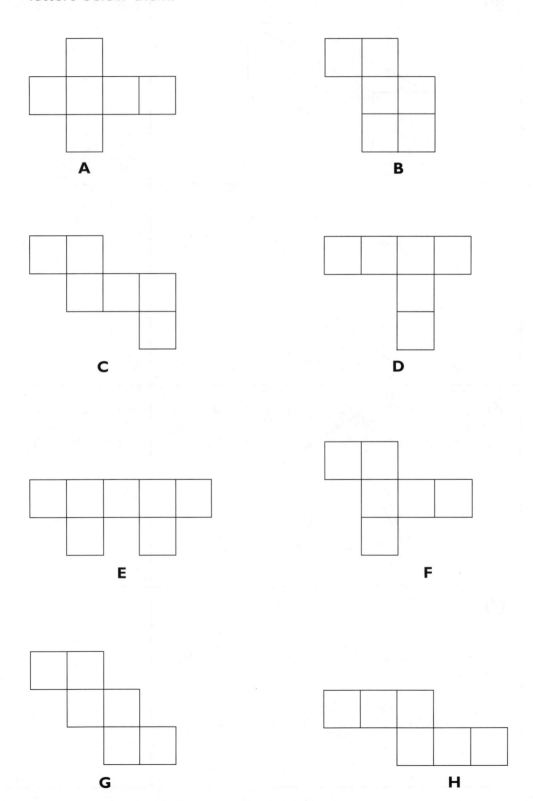

A

B

C

D

E

F

G

H

2. Which of the following can be folded to form a cuboid? Circle the letters below them.

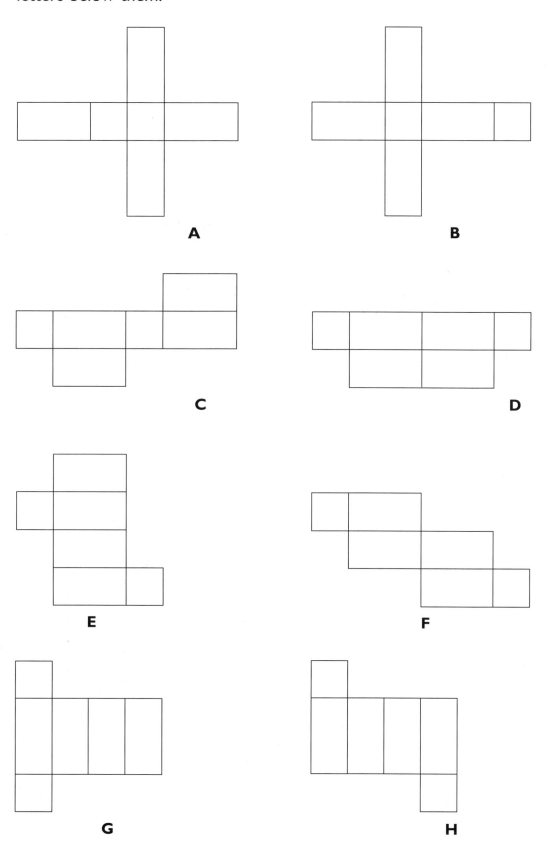

A

B

C

D

E

F

G

H

EXERCISE 6

1. This figure shows a solid.

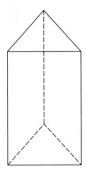

Which of the following can be a net of the solid?
Circle the letters below them.

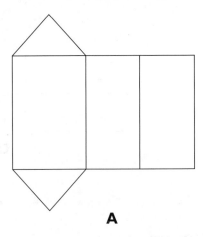

A

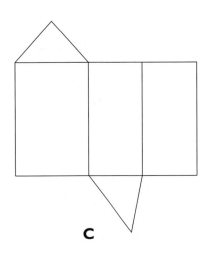

C

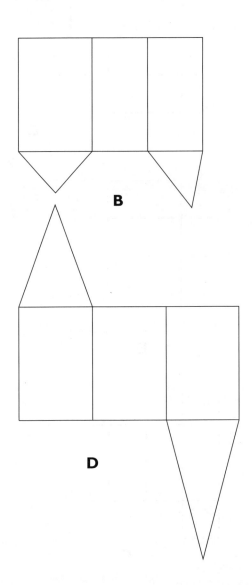

B

D

2. This figure shows a solid.

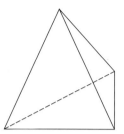

Which of the following can be a net of the solid?
Circle the letters below them.

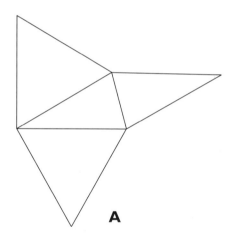

A

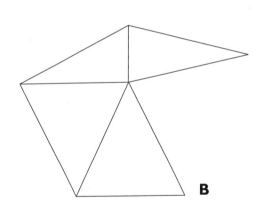

B

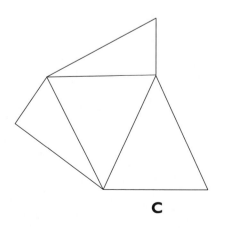

C

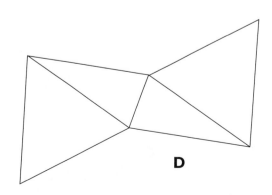

D

3. This figure shows a solid.

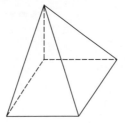

Which of the following can be a net of the solid?
Circle the letters below them.

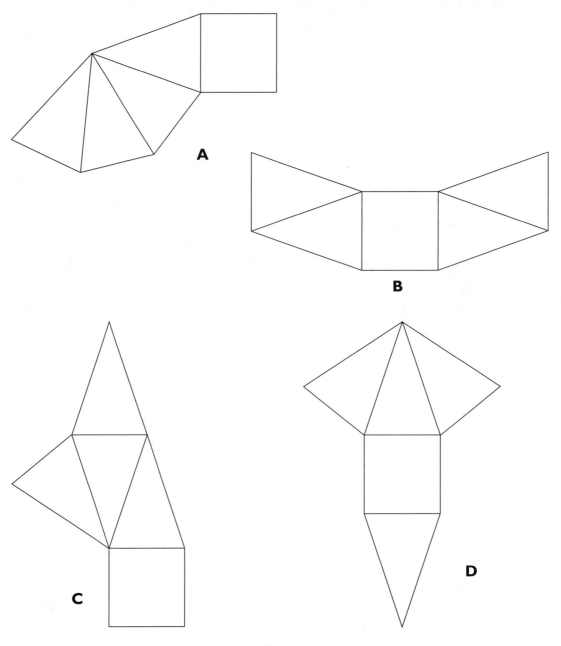

A

B

C

D

EXERCISE 7

1. This is a net of a solid.

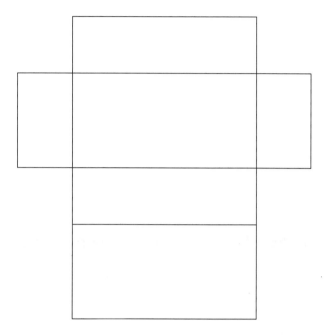

Which one of the following solids can be formed by the net? Circle the letter below it.

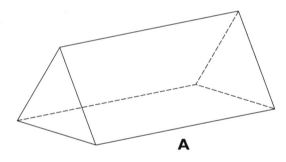

A

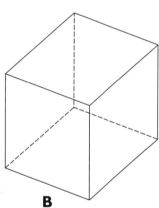

B

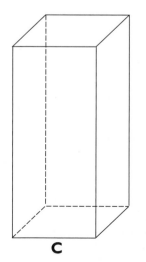

C

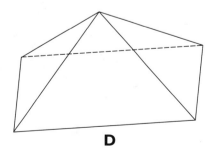

D

2. This is a net of a solid.

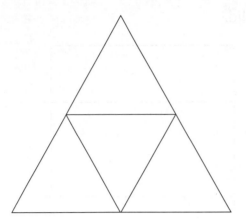

Which one of the following solids can be formed by the net? Circle the letter below it.

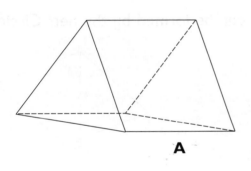

A

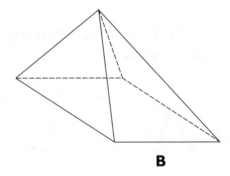

B

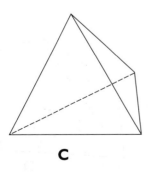

C

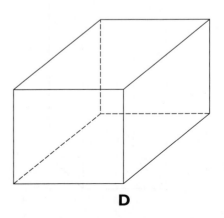

D

3. This is a net of a solid.

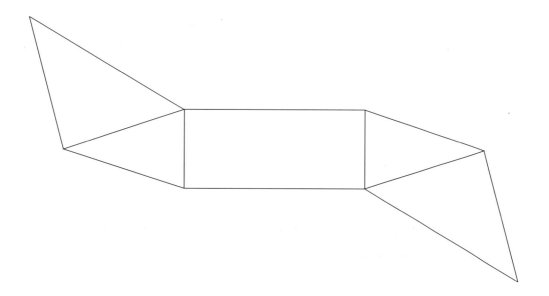

Which one of the following solids can be formed by the net? Circle the letter below it.

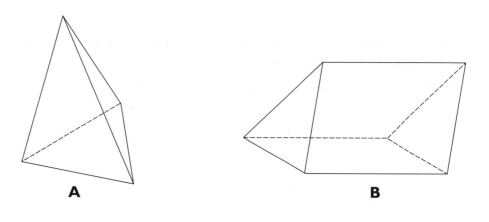

A

B

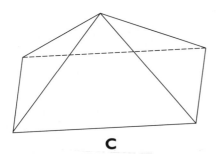

C

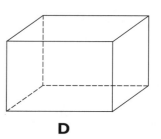

D

EXERCISE 8

1. 42 boys and 63 girls take part in an art competition.
    (a) Find the ratio of the number of boys to the number of girls.

    (b) Find the ratio of the number of boys to the number of girls to the total number of children.

2. Peter, Henry and John shared $345 among them. Peter received $45, Henry received $75 and John received the rest.
    (a) Find the ratio of Peter's share to Henry's share to John's share.

    (b) Find the ratio of John's share to the total amount of money.

3. The table shows the weights of three packages.

Package	Weight
A	6 kg
B	8 kg
C	12 kg

Write each of the following ratios in its simplest form.
(a) Weight of A : Weight of B

=

(b) Weight of A : Weight of C

=

(c) Weight of B : Weight of C

=

(d) Weight of A : Weight of B : Weight of C

=

4. Write each ratio in its simplest form.

(a) 20 : 15 =
(b) 16 : 48 =
(c) 10 : 30 : 24 =
(d) 60 : 40 : 80 =

EXERCISE 9

1. The weights of packages P and Q are in the ratio 6 : 5.

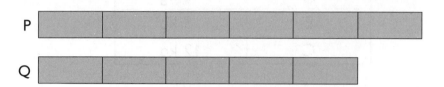

(a) What fraction of the weight of P is the weight of Q?

The weight of Q is [   ] of the weight of P.

(b) What fraction of the total weight of P and Q is the weight of P?

The weight of P is [   ] of the total weight of P and Q.

(c) Express the weight of P as a fraction of the weight of Q.

The weight of P is [   ] of the weight of Q.

2. The ratio of Paul's savings to Randy's savings is 2 : 3.

(a) Paul's savings is [   ] of Randy's savings.

(b) Randy's savings is [   ] of Paul's savings.

3. The ratio of the number of men to the number of women to the number of children at a concert is 4 : 2 : 3.

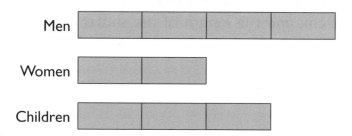

(a) Express the number of children as a fraction of the total number of men and women.

(b) How many times as many men as women are there?

4. Meihua's height is $\frac{5}{7}$ of Sumin's height.

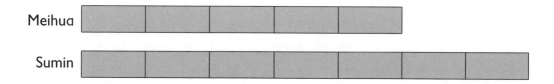

(a) Express Sumin's height as a fraction of Meihua's height.

(b) What is the ratio of Sumin's height to Meihua's height?

EXERCISE 10

1.   The lengths of three ribbons are in the ratio 3 : 5 : 7. If the length of the longest ribbon is 42 cm, find the length of the shortest ribbon.

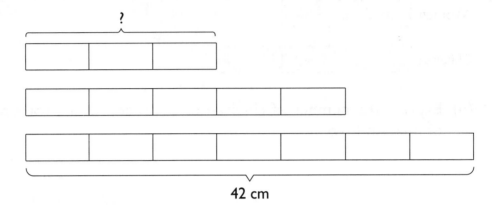

2. The number of male teachers is $\frac{2}{3}$ of the number of female teachers in a school. If there are 75 teachers altogether, how many more female teachers than male teachers are there?

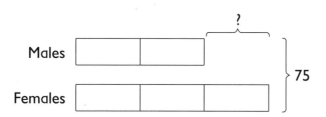

EXERCISE 11

1. The ratio of the number of cars to the number of vans is 2 : 1. The ratio of the number of vans to the number of motorcycles is 3 : 5.

   (a) Find the ratio of the number of cars to the number of vans to the number of motorcycles.

   Cars

   Vans

   Motorcycles

   Number of vans = 3 units
   Number of cars = ? units

   (b) If there are 25 motorcycles, how many cars are there?

2. $\frac{1}{2}$ of David's money is $\frac{2}{3}$ of Henry's money.

   (a) Express David's money as a fraction of Henry's money.

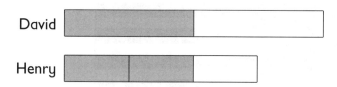

   (b) If David has $60 more than Henry, how much money do they have altogether?

EXERCISE 12

1. The ratio of the length to the width of our national flag is 5 : 3.

(a) Complete the following table.

Length (cm)	Width (cm)
5	3
	15
	30
	45

(b) If the length is 120 cm, find the width.

(c) If the length is 150 cm, find the width.

2.   Sharon mixed meat with potatoes in the ratio 7 : 3 to make 4 kg of meat loaf. How much meat did she use?

3.   Connie mixed lime juice, lemon juice and water in the ratio 3 : 6 : 7 to make 8 liters of drink. How many liters of lime juice did she use?

EXERCISE 13

1. The ratio of the number of Meili's stickers to Suhua's is 3 : 7. Suhua has 32 more stickers than Meili. If Suhua gives $\frac{1}{4}$ of her stickers to Meili, what will be the new ratio of the number of Meili's stickers to Suhua's?

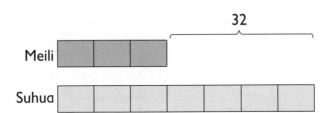

2. Both Joe and Conner have the same amount of money. If Joe gives $\frac{1}{3}$ of his money to Conner, what will be the ratio of Joe's money to Conner's money?

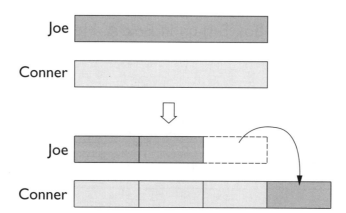

EXERCISE 14

1. The ratio of the number of beads in Box A to that in Box B was 6 : 5.

    After $\frac{1}{2}$ of the beads in Box A were moved to Box B, there were

    30 more beads in Box B than in Box A. How many beads were there
    in Box A at first?

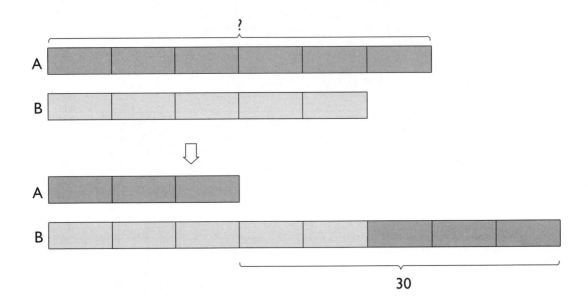

2. The ratio of John's money to Peter's money was 4 : 7 at first. After John spent $\frac{1}{2}$ of his money and Peter spent $60, Peter had twice as much money as John. How much money did John have at first?

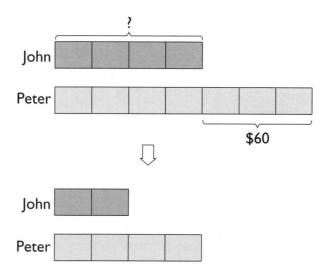

3. Susan and Mary each had 50 carnival tickets at first . After Susan gave some tickets to Mary, the number of Susan's tickets was $\frac{2}{3}$ of the number of Mary's tickets. How many tickets did Susan give to Mary?

Susan [|]

Mary [| |] } 100

The total number of tickets remained unchanged.

36

REVIEW 1

Write the answers in the boxes.

1. Write down a common multiple of 6 and 10.

2. Find the value of each of the following:

   (a) $(15 + 35) \div 5 \times 5$

   (b) $120 \div 12 + 7 \times 8$

3. Arrange the fractions in increasing order.

   (a) $2\frac{1}{4}$, $\frac{5}{4}$, $1\frac{11}{12}$, $\frac{12}{4}$

   (b) $1\frac{2}{3}$, $\frac{45}{8}$, $1\frac{7}{8}$, $\frac{18}{6}$

4. What is the missing number in each ■?

   (a) $1\frac{3}{8} \ell = ■$ ml

   (b) $4\frac{3}{4}$ kg = ■ kg ■ g

5. Find the missing number in each ■.

   (a) $3 : 8 = ■ : 24$

   (b) $5 : 6 : 3 = 25 : ■ : 15$

   (c) $4 : ■ = 12 : 21$

   (d) $■ : 5 : 8 = 24 : 20 : 32$

6. The average price of three mugs is $4. One of the mugs costs $p and another mug costs $3. Express the price of the third mug in terms of p in the simplest form.

7. Cindy's weight is 38 kg. Heather is 6 kg heavier than Cindy. Find their average weight.

8. There are 3 times as many boys as girls in a school band. If there are 12 girls, how many more boys than girls are there?

9. A cake costs $1.20. It costs twice as much as a pie. Find the cost of 3 pies and 2 cakes.

10. Water flows out of a tank at the rate of 400 ml per minute. How long will it take for 7.2 liters of water to flow out of the tank?

11. Skylar had 2.72 kg of honey. She used 0.27 kg of honey a day for 8 days. How many kilograms of honey did she have left?

12. 720 children took part in a fire drill. $\frac{5}{8}$ of them were boys. How many girls were there?

13. $\frac{2}{3}$ of a group of children were girls. $\frac{4}{5}$ of the girls were girl scouts. What fraction of the children were girl scouts?

14. Molly had $80. She gave $\frac{3}{4}$ of it to her mother and $\frac{1}{2}$ of the remaining to her brother. How much money did she have left?

15. James spent $\frac{2}{5}$ of his money and saved the rest. If he spent $630, how much did he save?

16. The capacities of 3 buckets are in the ratio 3 : 2 : 4. If the total capacity of the 3 buckets is 36 liters, find the capacity of the smallest bucket.

17. Russell's weight is $\frac{3}{4}$ of Brooke's weight. Find the ratio of Russell's weight to Brooke's weight.

18. The ratio of the length of String A to the length of String B is 1 : 3.

    (a) How many times is String B as long as String A?

    (b) Find the ratio of the length of String A to the total length of Strings A and B.

19. The ratio of the number of girls to the number of boys in a stamp club is 5 : 7.
    (a) Express the number of boys as a fraction of the number of girls.

    (b) Express the number of boys as a fraction of the total number of boys and girls.

20. There are 3 times as many adults as children at a book fair.
    (a) What is the ratio of the number of adults to the total number of people at the book fair?

    (b) What fraction of the people are children?

    (c) If there are 207 children, how many people are there altogether?

21. In a school, 3 out of every 5 students wear glasses. If 220 boys and 260 girls wear glasses, find the total number of students in the school.

22. The ratio of the length of a rectangle to its width is 4 : 3. If the length of the rectangle is 16 cm, find its perimeter.

23. The ratio of the length of a rectangle to its width is 7 : 4. If the perimeter of the rectangle is 44 cm, find its area.

24. The ratio of the length of a rectangle to its width is 5 : 3. If the length is increased by 2 cm, the ratio becomes 2 : 1.

    (a) Find the length of the rectangle before the increase.

    (b) Find the area of the rectangle after the increase.

25. Find the area of the shaded triangle.

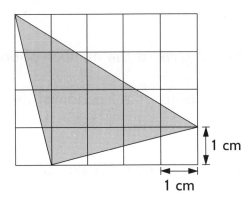

1 cm

1 cm

26. The figure is made up of a square and two triangles. Find its area.

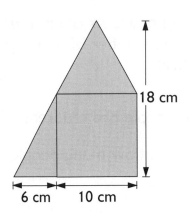

18 cm

6 cm   10 cm

27. Eugene bought 27 comics and 12 magazines for $126. If 3 comics cost as much as 2 magazines, find the cost of each comic.

28. David spent $\frac{1}{3}$ of his money on books. He spent another $\frac{1}{6}$ of it on stationery and $50 on a radio. If he had $100 left, how much money did he have at first?

29. Alice, Ben and Carol shared a sum of money. Alice received $\frac{1}{5}$ of the money. The rest of the money was divided between Ben and Carol in the ratio 1 : 3. If Carol received $6 more than Alice, how much money did Ben receive?

---

30. The average weight of 3 containers A, B and C is 3.2 kg. Container A is twice as heavy as Container B. Container B is 400 g heavier than Container C. Find the weight of Container C.

EXERCISE 15

1. Express each of the following as a percentage.

(a)

$$\frac{25}{100} =$$

25 out of 100

(b)

$$\frac{20}{50} =$$

20 out of 50

(c)

84 out of 300

$$\frac{84}{300} =$$

2. Write each fraction as a percentage.

(a)

$$\frac{3}{4} =$$

(b)

$$\frac{1}{5} =$$

(c)

$$\frac{7}{8} =$$

3. Write each fraction as a percentage.

(a) $\dfrac{48}{100}$ =	(b) $\dfrac{6}{10}$ =
(c) $\dfrac{3}{5}$ =	(d) $\dfrac{15}{75}$ =
(e) $\dfrac{6}{40}$ =	(f) $\dfrac{5}{8}$ =
(g) $\dfrac{60}{80}$ =	(h) $\dfrac{168}{700}$ =

EXERCISE 16

1. Express each percentage as a fraction in its simplest form.

(a) 2% =	(b) 15% =
(c) 24% =	(d) 45% =
(e) 60% =	(f) 74% =

2. Express each decimal as a percentage.

(a) 0.3 =	(b) 0.08 =

(c) 0.67 =	(d) 0.004 =
(e) 0.025 =	(f) 0.385 =

3. Express each percentage as a decimal.

(a) 2% =	(b) 7% =
(c) 10% =	(d) 80% =
(e) 25% =	(f) 99% =

EXERCISE 17

1. There are 25 girls, 18 boys and 7 adults on a bus. What percentage of the people on the bus are adults?

---

2. Ben, Mingli and Samy shared $180. Ben received $45, Mingli received $63 and Samy received the rest. What percentage of the money did Samy receive?

3. Duncan spent $480 on a television set and had $320 left. What percentage of his money did he spend on the television set?

---

4. 400 students were asked to choose their favorite games. 26% of them chose baseball, 12% basketball, 10% volleyball and the rest chose soccer. How many students chose soccer as their favorite game?

EXERCISE 18

1. Aminah had $120. She spent 20% of the money on food and 25% of the remaining on clothes.

    (a) What percentage of the money did she have left?

    (b) How much money did she have left?

2. There were 1500 people at a concert. 55% of them were men, 20% of the remainder were women and the rest were children. How many children were there?

EXERCISE 19

1. 5000 people visited a book fair in the first week. The number of visitors was increased by 10% in the second week. How many people visited the book fair in the second week?

2. The usual price of a washing machine was $400. At a sale, the price was reduced by 25%. What was the price of the washing machine at the sale?

3. Kendall bought a vase that cost $450. In addition, she had to pay 3% sales tax. How much did she pay for the vase?

---

4. There were 24 boys and 20 girls in a chess club last year. This year the number of boys in the club was increased by 25% but the number of girls was decreased by 10%. Find the overall increase or decrease in the membership of the club.

EXERCISE 20

1. Express 80 cm as a percentage of 2 m.

---

2. Express 750 g as a percentage of 1.5 kg.

---

3. Express 120 ml as a percentage of 0.8 ℓ.

4. Express $15 as a percentage of $12.

---

5. Express 1.2 km as a percentage of 300 m.

---

6. Express 2.5 kg as a percentage of 2 kg.

EXERCISE 21

1.   The usual price of a calculator was $25. It was sold for $19.
      (a) How much discount was given?

      (b) Express the discount as a percentage of the usual price.

---

2.   Mrs. Bode's monthly salary was increased from $1200 to $1500.
      (a) Find the increase in her monthly salary.

      (b) By what percentage was her monthly salary increased?

3.   The mathematics club had 24 members last year. It has 36 members this year. By what percentage was the number of members increased?

4.   On Sunday, there were 1200 spectators at an air show. On Monday, there were 900 spectators at the show. By what percentage was the number of spectators decreased?

EXERCISE 22

1. There are 42 boys and 24 girls in a chess club. How many percent more boys than girls are there?

---

2. There are 400 students in a school hall. 240 of them are boys. How many percent more boys than girls are there?

3. A cook used 6 gal of cooking oil last month. She used 15% less this month. How much cooking oil did she use this month?

4. Scott earned $600 in January. He earned 14% more in February than in January. How much did he earn in February?

EXERCISE 23

1. John had $50. He spent 60% of the money on clothes and 60% of the remainder on food.

    (a) How much more did he spend on clothes than on food?

    (b) How many percent more did he spend on clothes than on food?

2. John has $400. Peter has 20% more money than John and twice as much as Henry.
    (a) How much money do they have altogether?

    (b) What percentage of John's money is Henry's money?

EXERCISE 24

1. 20% of Menon's books are comic books. If Menon has 52 comic books, how many books does he have altogether?

2. Sulin's savings is 75% of Meifen's savings. If Sulin saves $300, how much does Meifen save?

3. Peter spent 60% of his money on a book and had $18 left. How much money did he have at first?

4. Gopal gave away 25% of his stamps and had 450 stamps left. How many stamps did he give away?

EXERCISE 25

1.   A dress was sold for $42 after a 30% discount. What was the usual price of the dress?

___

2.   The price of a television set was increased by 10% to $2420. What was the price before the increase?

3. In a school choir, the number of boys was increased by 20% to 60 and the number of girls was decreased by 20% to 60. Find the overall increase or decrease in the membership of the choir.

EXERCISE 26

1. 2300 people visited a book fair on Sunday. This was 15% more than the number of visitors on Saturday. How many visitors were there on Saturday?

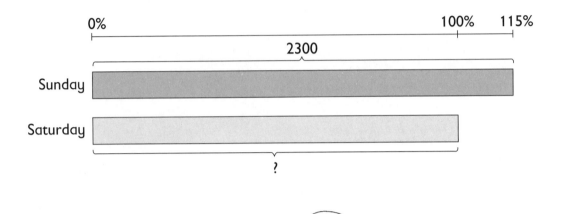

Take the number on Saturday as 100%.
The number on Sunday was 115%.

2. Mary spent 40% of her money on a handbag and 40% of the remainder on a pair of shoes. She had $90 left. How much money did she have at first?

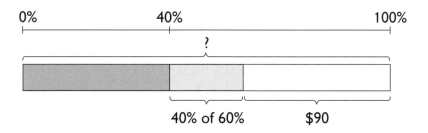

100% − 40% = 60%

The remainder is 60% of her money.

3. 30% of Elliot's stamps are Canadian stamps. The rest are U.S. stamps. If Elliot has 500 more U.S. stamps than Canadian stamps, how many stamps does he have altogether?

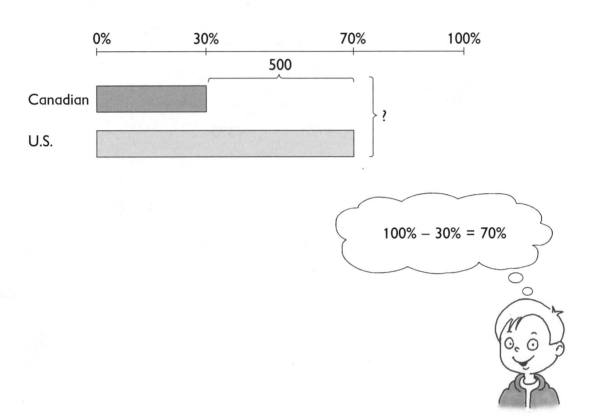

100% − 30% = 70%

4. There are 25% more girls than boys in a club. If there are 36 more girls than boys, how many boys are there?

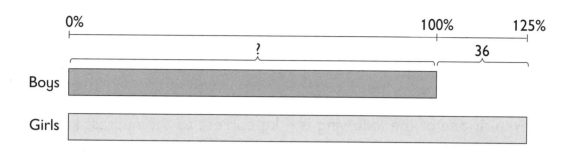

Take the number of boys as 100%.
The number of girls is 125%.

REVIEW 2

Write the answers in the boxes.

1. Given that $135 \times 37 = 4995$, find the value of 1350×3700.

2. Which one of the following is 4 kg correct to the nearest kilogram?

   3.399 kg,   3.499 kg,   3.49 kg,   3.59 kg

3. Write down two common factors of 24 and 32.

4. What is the missing number in each ■?

   (a) 7:40 a.m. is ■ h ■ min after 12:00 midnight.

   (b) 8:20 p.m. is ■ h ■ min before 12:00 midnight.

5. What is the missing number in each ■?

   (a) $34.25 \times ■ = 3425$

   (b) $\dfrac{576}{■} = 57.6$

6. Write $\dfrac{9}{100} + 3$ as a decimal.

7. Express each of the following as a percentage.

   (a) $\dfrac{16}{200}$

   (b) 0.046

8. There are 40 students in a class. $\dfrac{7}{8}$ of them are girls. $\dfrac{3}{5}$ of the girls walk to school. How many girls walk to school?

9. Mrs. Long bought a cake. She kept $\frac{1}{4}$ of it and divided the rest into 2 equal parts. What fraction of a whole cake is each part?

10. Tyler has 4 times as much money as Ryan. Find the ratio of Ryan's money to Tyler's money.

11. $\frac{2}{5}$ of the workers in a factory are females. Find the ratio of the number of male workers to the number of female workers.

12. The ratio of Joe's weight to Colin's is 2 : 3. Colin's weight is 36 kg.
    (a) Express Joe's weight as a fraction of Colin's weight.

    (b) If Joe gains 3 kg, what will be the new ratio of Joe's weight to Colin's?

13. Melissa mixed 400 g of cashew nuts with 600 g of peanuts to make 1 kg of mixed nuts.
    (a) Find the ratio of the weight of cashew nuts to the weight of peanuts.

    (b) If she wants to make 500 g of mixed nuts by mixing cashew nuts and peanuts in the same ratio, how many grams of cashew nuts does she need?

14. What percentage of the circles are shaded?

15. The usual price of a fan was $75. A discount of 20% was given during a sale. Find the sale price of the fan.

16. A man deposited $840 in a bank for 1 year. If the bank paid 4% interest per year, how much interest did he receive?

17. The membership of a club was increased from 40 to 50. By what percentage was the membership increased?

18. Brian saves 20% of his monthly salary. If his monthly salary is increased from $1200 to $1500, how much more can he save each month?

19. Bonita has 15% more stamps than Jessica. If Bonita has 150 more stamps than Jessica, how many stamps do they have altogether?

20. 20% of the marbles in a box are red. 40% are yellow and the rest are green. If there are 80 green marbles, how many marbles are there altogether?

21. Jared spends 20% of his monthly salary on food and 30% of the remainder on transport. He saves the rest. What percentage of the salary does he save?

22. Lily earns $20 for 8 hours of part-time work.

    (a) How much is she paid per hour?

    (b) How much can she earn if she works 10 hours?

    (c) How many hours does she have to work to earn $50?

23. A merry-go-round makes 25 revolutions in 5 minutes. How long will it take to make 30 revolutions?

24. A piece of wire is bent to form a shape like this:

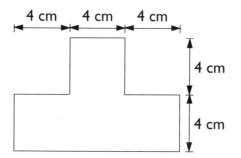

Find the length of the wire.

25. ABCD is a square of side 12 cm. Find the area of the shaded part.

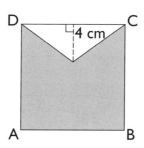

26. Use the given shape to make a tessellation in the space provided.

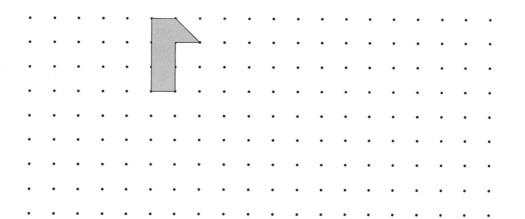

EXERCISE 27

1. Complete the following table.

	Distance	Time	Speed
(a)	150 km	3 h	$\dfrac{150}{3}$ =
(b)	450 km	6 h	
(c)		2 h	45 km/h
(d)	330 km		60 km/h

EXERCISE 28

1.   A van traveled 216 km in 4 hours. Find its average speed in km/h.

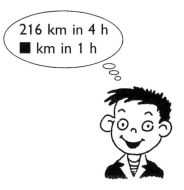

216 km in 4 h
■ km in 1 h

2.   David swam 800 m in 20 minutes. Find his average speed in m/min.

3.   A car traveled at an average speed of 80 km/h for 5 hours. What was the distance traveled?

4. Jerome took 15 minutes to walk from his house to a community center. His average speed was 60 m/min. Find the distance between Jerome's house and the community center.

5. A train traveled 30 mi at an average speed of 60 mi/h. Find the time taken for the trip.

6. A car traveled from Town A to Town B at an average speed of 80 km/h. How long did the trip take?

EXERCISE 29

1. Shawn takes 2 minutes to cycle 800 m.
    (a) Find his average speed.
    (b) If he continues to cycle for another 5 minutes at the same
        average speed, how much further will he travel? Give your answer
        in kilometers.

2. Tyler took 2 hours to drive from Town A to Town B which were
    150 km apart.
    (a) Find his average speed.
    (b) How many hours would he take to drive from Town B to Town A
        if the average speed for the return trip was 60 km/h?

3.   Miguel walked 910 m from home to his office. His average speed was 70 m/min. He left home at 7:30 a.m. At what time did he arrive at his office?

---

4.   Amanda took 6 minutes to walk from her school to the nearest train station. Her average speed was 80 m/min. How long would she take if her average speed was 60 m/min?

EXERCISE 30

1. Meihua jogged for $\frac{1}{2}$ hour at 6 km/h. She jogged for another $\frac{1}{4}$ hour at 8 km/h. What distance did she jog altogether?

---

2. In a 9-km walkathon, Susan walked at an average speed of 6 km/h for the first 3 km and at an average speed of 4 km/h for the remaining distance. How much time did she take for the walkathon?

3. Ryan and David both cycled from Town X to Town Y. They started at the same time. After cycling for 4 hours, Ryan completed the trip but David still had 2 km to cycle. If Ryan's average speed was 10 km/h, find David's average speed for the 4 hours.

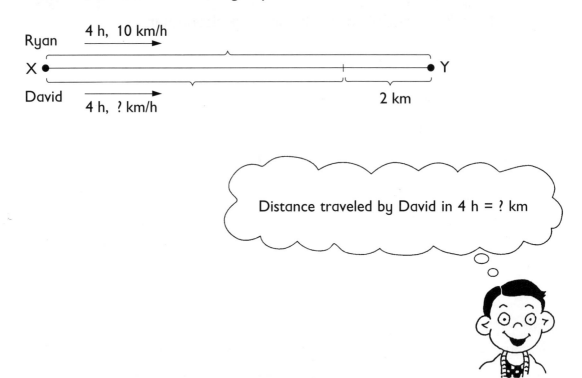

Distance traveled by David in 4 h = ? km

4.

A car traveled from Town X to Town Y at an average speed of 88 km/h. Then it traveled from Town Y to Town Z at an average speed of 64 km/h.

(a) Find the total time taken.

(b) Find the average speed for the whole trip.

5. Daniel took 1 hour to drive from Town A to Town B at an average speed of 70 km/h. Then he took 2 hours to drive from Town B to Town C at an average speed of 64 km/h.

(a) Find the total distance traveled.

(b) Find the average speed for the whole trip.

EXERCISE 31

1. Nicholas drove from Town P to Town Q. He took 2 hours to travel $\frac{3}{5}$ of the trip. He took another 1 hour to travel the remaining trip at an average speed of 60 km/h. Find his average speed for the whole trip.

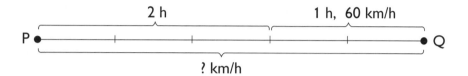

? km/h

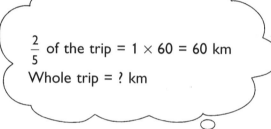

$\frac{2}{5}$ of the trip = 1 × 60 = 60 km

Whole trip = ? km

2. Ali cycled from Town A to Town B. He covered $\frac{1}{5}$ of the trip in the first hour and $\frac{1}{3}$ of the trip in the second hour. He took 2 hours to cycle the remaining 14 km. Find his average speed for the whole trip.

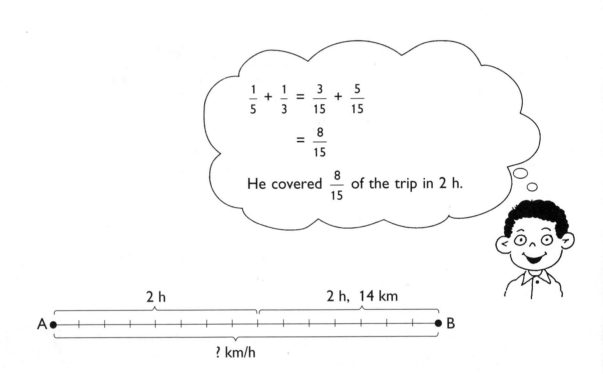

$$\frac{1}{5} + \frac{1}{3} = \frac{3}{15} + \frac{5}{15}$$

$$= \frac{8}{15}$$

He covered $\frac{8}{15}$ of the trip in 2 h.

2 h   2 h, 14 km

A •———————————————————• B

? km/h

REVIEW 3

Write the answers in the boxes.

1. In 20.165, the value of the digit 5 is equal to 5 × ■. What is the missing number in the ■?

2. Write down the multiples of 7 between 20 and 30.

3. Which one of the following numbers is nearest to 70?
   69.098,   69.307,   69.48,   69.51

4. What is the missing number in each ■?

   (a) $0.024 \times$ ■ $= 24$

   (b) $8 \times \dfrac{2}{3} = \dfrac{2}{3} + \dfrac{2}{3} +$ ■ $\times \dfrac{2}{3}$

5. Express $\dfrac{1}{4} + \dfrac{2}{5}$ as a percentage.

6. Emily has 800 sticks of chicken satay. She sells all of them at 30 cents each. How much money does she receive?

7. For every 5 pens sold, a shopkeeper earns $2.50. How many pens must he sell to earn $20?

8. The capacity of a container is 3 liters. It contains $1\dfrac{2}{5}$ liters of water. How much more water is needed to fill up the container?

9. A mug can hold 400 ml of water. A jug can hold 1 ℓ 200 ml of water. What is the ratio of the capacity of the mug to the capacity of the jug?

85

10. Paige mixed lemon juice with water in the ratio 2 : 3 to make 2 liters of lemonade. How much lemon juice did she use? Give your answer in liters.

11. A machine can make 60 toy soldiers in $\frac{1}{2}$ hour. At this rate, how many toy soldiers can it make in 10 minutes?

12. Tommy is cycling at a speed of 16 km/h. How many minutes will he take to cycle 4 km?

13. Alyssa saved $46. Renee saved 3 times as much as Alyssa. Betty saved $40 less than Renee. On the average, how much did each girl save?

14. Mary's height is $\frac{6}{7}$ of Jane's height. If Jane is 15 cm taller than Mary, what is Jane's height?

15. William had $4500. He spent $\frac{2}{5}$ of the money on a computer and $\frac{1}{4}$ of the remainder on books. How much did he spend on books?

16. In a walkathon, $\frac{5}{8}$ of the participants are men, $\frac{1}{4}$ are women and the rest are children. What percentage of the participants are children?

17. The usual price of a computer was $2800. It was sold for $2380 after a discount was given. How many percent discount was given?

18. Jacob took 3 hours to drive from Town A to Town B at an average speed of 80 km/h. On his way back, he drove at an average speed of 60 km/h. If he left Town B at 1:00 p.m., what time did he return to Town A?

19. Chelsea bought 5 books for $21. If the average cost of 2 of the books is $7.80, find the average cost of the other 3 books.

20. Mary took 2 days to read $\frac{1}{3}$ of a book. She took 6 days to read the remaining pages at the rate of 40 pages per day. On the average, how many pages did she read in one day?

21. The bar graph shows the number of families with 0, 1, 2, 3 and 4 children in a neighborhood. Study the graph and answer the questions which follow.

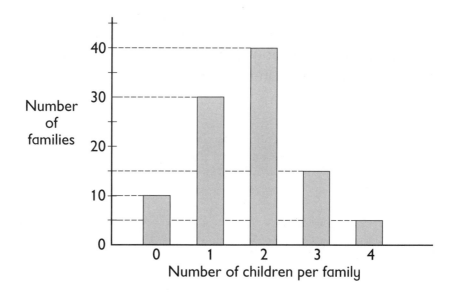

(a) How many families have 2 or more children?

(b) Find the ratio of the number of families with 2 or more children to the number of families with less than 2 children.

22. Kristi spent $\frac{2}{5}$ of her money on 6 mangoes and 7 pears. Each mango cost $2.50 and each pear cost $0.80. How much money did she have left?

23. The ratio of the number of boys to the number of girls in a hall was 3 : 2 at first. After 30 boys left the hall, the ratio became 2 : 3. How many boys were there in the hall at first ?

24. Calvin's monthly salary is $1200. In January, he spends 80% of the salary and saves the rest. In February, he spends 10% less than what he spends in January. How much does he save in February?

---

25. John and Peter traveled from Town P to Town Q. Peter left Town P at 8:30 a.m. John left Town P 1 hour later. They both reached Town Q at 1:30 p.m. If Peter's average speed for the trip was 60 km/h, find John's average speed.

REVIEW 4

Write the answers in the boxes.

1. What fraction of the circle is shaded?

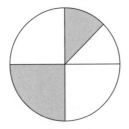

2. What is the missing number in each ■?

    (a) $\dfrac{3}{5} + \dfrac{3}{5} + \dfrac{3}{5} + \dfrac{3}{5} = ■ \times \dfrac{1}{5}$

    (b) $\dfrac{5}{8} + ■ = 1$

    (c) $4\dfrac{3}{5} = 4 + ■$

    (d) $5 = \dfrac{■}{5}$

3. Which one of the following is the same as $\dfrac{3}{4}$?

    $\dfrac{4}{3}$, $\dfrac{5}{12}$, $\dfrac{6}{8}$, $\dfrac{8}{12}$

4. Write each fraction as a decimal correct to 2 decimal places.

    (a) $\dfrac{3}{7} =$ ⬚   (b) $2\dfrac{4}{9} =$ ⬚

5. Find the value of each of the following in its simplest form.

    (a) $1\dfrac{3}{4} + 2\dfrac{7}{8} =$ ⬚   (b) $4\dfrac{5}{12} - 2\dfrac{3}{4} =$ ⬚

    (c) $\dfrac{5}{8} \times 4 =$ ⬚   (d) $\dfrac{3}{10} \times \dfrac{5}{12} =$ ⬚

    (e) $\dfrac{3}{8} \div 6 =$ ⬚   (f) $\dfrac{5}{9} \div 5 =$ ⬚

6. Which one of the following is the smallest?

$\frac{3}{4}$,   0.81, $\frac{11}{8}$,   65%

7. $\frac{2}{3}$ of a number is 0.3. What is the number?

8. Express 36% as a fraction in its simplest form.

9. Find the value of 45% of 6 km.

10. Mr. Reed gave $\frac{3}{5}$ of his money to his wife. He gave $\frac{1}{4}$ of the remainder to his son. What fraction of his money did he give to his son?

11. At a sale, James bought a bicycle at $\frac{7}{9}$ of its usual price. The bicycle cost $28 less than its usual price. How much did James pay for the bicycle?

12. Dorothy had $850. She gave $400 to her parents. Then she spent 40% of the remainder and saved the rest. How much did she save?

13. 60% of the vehicles owned by a transport company are trucks, 15% are vans and the rest are buses. If there are 10 buses, how many trucks are there?

14. $\frac{2}{5}$ of the people at an exhibition are men, $\frac{3}{8}$ of them are women and the rest are children. Find the ratio of the number of men to the number of women to the number of children.

15. The number of Adam's stamps was $\frac{5}{6}$ of the number of Peter's stamps at first. After Adam gave away 40 stamps, the ratio of the number of Adam's stamps to that of Peter's was 1 : 2. How many stamps did Adam have at first?

16. Danny jogged at an average speed of 12 km/h for 20 minutes. What distance did he jog?

17. The figure is made up of a rectangle and two triangles. Find the area of the figure.

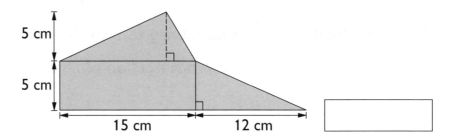

18. The line graph shows the number of bags Mr. Bush sold on 5 days.

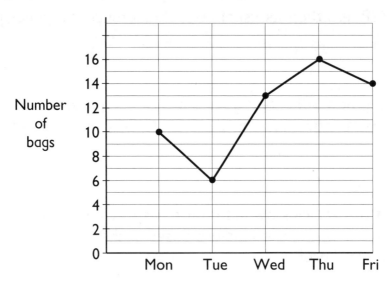

(a) How many bags did Mr. Bush sell on Wednesday?

(b) On which day did he sell the most number of bags?

(c) Find the average number of bags sold per day.

19.

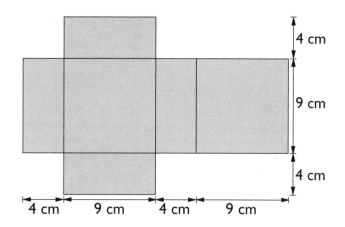

The figure shows a net of a cuboid. Find the total area of the 6 faces of the cuboid.

20. In each of the following, is the dotted line a line of symmetry of the figure?

(a)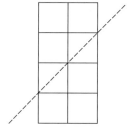

(b)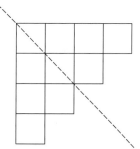

(c)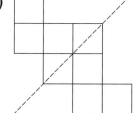

(d)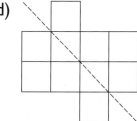

21. (a) Draw a square in which the length of the side is 6 cm.

(b) Draw a rhombus ABCD in which AB = 5 cm and $\angle$DAB = 50°.

22. Lacey had $10 more than Hannah. Lacey spent all her money on 12 plates while Hannah used all her money to buy 8 cups at $1.65 each and 4 plates. Find the cost of 1 plate.

---

23. John, David and Ben shared a sum of money. John received $\frac{1}{3}$ of the sum of money. David received twice as much money as Ben. If John received $36, how much money did Ben receive?

24. Bridget, Laura and Reagan shared a sum of money. Bridget's share was 40% of the money. Reagan's share was $4 more than Laura's. Laura's share was $16. How much money did they share altogether?

---

25. Thomas, took 3 hours to cycle from Town A to Town B. He cycled $\frac{3}{5}$ of the distance in the first 2 hours. He cycled the remaining distance in the third hour. If his average speed for the first part of the trip was 9 km/h, find his average speed for the last part of the trip.